BRITAIN'S COASTLINE

JEROME MONAHAN

MYRIAD
LONDON

South-East England

England's south-east coast features dockyards, coastal forts and castles – testament to a rich past bound up with the nation's frequent need to defend itself. In the 19th century its fishing villages were transformed into popular seaside resorts and became a magnet for ordinary Londoners. Today much of the south coast is still under siege, this time from the elements and rising sea levels, but this has often created beautiful beaches and spectacular cliffs that have long captured the imagination of artists and poets.

Whitstable *right*

Oysters remain central to the identity of Whitstable on the north Kent coast. Now a magnet for artists, Whitstable is enjoying something of a boom. This follows a period of neglect since its heyday in the 19th century when it was a popular seaside resort and boasted a thriving harbour (built 1832), a boatbuilding industry and fishing fleet. The oyster season lasts from September to April and each July the town holds an Oyster Festival. Neighbouring Herne Bay is another seaside resort enjoying a revival having recently secured a European Blue Flag in recognition of its clean beach. Herne Bay has wonderful late Victorian seaside architecture; its glorious bandstand has recently been restored and its brightly-coloured beach huts command eyewatering prices.

Rochester Castle *below*

The town of Rochester owes its development to its position at the mouth of the Medway where it joins the Thames. It is here that the Roman-built Watling Street that links London, Canterbury and Dover crosses the Medway. Its first castle was built in the reign of William I and was one of the earliest English castles to be built of stone. The imposing keep with its 113ft tower constructed from Kentish ragstone was built in the ninety-year period from 1127 when the castle was the responsibility of the Archbishops of Canterbury. The castle has endured a number of sieges over the centuries including one commanded by King John in 1215 during which the southern part of the keep suffered significant damage. Rochester Castle is now owned and maintained by English Heritage.

Margate *above*

A night-time view of the seafront at Margate shows off its bright lights reflected in the tide-damp sands that form the North Kent coast resort's major attraction. In the middle ages it was one of the "limbs" of the Cinque Port of Dover, enjoying privileges alongside the responsibility of providing ships capable of defending the country at time of war.

Rochester *left*

The Medway town is proud of its associations with Charles Dickens who lived nearby at Gads Hill Place, Higham. Every year two festivals celebrate this link – the Summer Dickens Festival in June and the Dickensian Christmas Festival in December. Descriptions of Rochester appear in *The Pickwick Papers* and the town is the inspiration for "Cloisterham" in *The Mystery of Edwin Drood*. Satis House, the home of Miss Havisham in *Great Expectations*, was based on Restoration House, in Crow Lane.

Dover *above*

Dover was the most prominent of the five Cinque Ports created in the mid 11th century during the reign of Edward the Confessor and charged with "ship service" – providing naval vessels and men to protect England in exchange for many civic privileges including running their own judicial affairs. The history of Dover Castle dates back to pre-Roman times as proved by the remains of earthworks discovered by archaeologists. The current fortress was mainly laid out in Henry II's reign but underwent significant rebuilding during the Napoleonic Wars when there was a significant threat of invasion.

White Cliffs *right*

For the British, the White Cliffs of Dover are full of symbolism, defining the country's independence from Continental Europe and forming a natural bastion at times of threatened invasion. Created over a period of 80 million years following the last Ice Age, they have been designated a Site of Special Scientific Interest thanks to the specific plant, animal and insect life that thrives on the cliffsides and tops. The cliffs provide a good roosting place for a variety of birds including black-tipped gulls, fulmars and kittiwakes and are also a regular stopping-off point for migrating birds.

Camber Sands *above*

The only sand dune system in East Sussex is to be found at
Camber and it provides an important habitat for many species
of animals and plants. Camber Sands has seen many wrecks and
has been used as a location for a number of films, including the
Dunkirk evacuation beaches in *The Battle Of Britain* and the
Sahara in *Carry On – Follow That Camel*.

Dungeness *below*

Dungeness is an other-worldly spot on the Kent coast where
extensive shingle deposits have created an extraordinary
landscape. Apart from the two nearby nuclear power stations,
the only other major buildings in the area are two lighthouses.
The 1901 lighthouse is now a tourist attraction. The wooden
fishing hut called Prospect Cottage was owned by the artist and
film director Derek Jarman who created a much-visited garden
using local hardy plants, pebbles and beachcombing "finds".
There is a 2,500-acre RSPB nature reserve at Dungeness. This
beautiful spot can be reached by the miniature steam trains of
the Romney, Hythe and Dymchurch Railway.

Hastings *above*

Hastings was one of the original Cinque Ports. Its position as a centre of maritime power was undermined
in the 18th century due to a combination of storms that washed the town into the sea and repeated raids
by the French. Hastings lost out to other coastal towns due to its lack of a harbour and its boats are still
forced to moor on the beach. An attempt in the late 19th century to build a harbour ran into financial
problems and the construction work that had been completed was then blown up in the Second World
War as a defensive measure. Hastings is famous for its curiously shaped Victorian "net shops" used by the
town's fishermen for storage. The shops were tall and narrow to avoid ground taxes.

Beachy Head *right*

The chalk headland at Beachy Head rises to over 535ft (163m) above sea level. At this point the undulating cliffs form themselves into a number of headlands known as the Seven Sisters. This line of cliffs is receding at approximately 2-3ins per year due to coastal erosion; major rock falls often occur after heavy rain or rough seas. The 1902 Matthews Lighthouse is the third to have been built on or near the cliffs to safeguard shipping.

Brighton *below*

Brighton has long been a fashionable destination – a pattern established when the Prince Regent (later George IV) made it a favourite spot in the 1790s. He commissioned Thomas Nash to design the exotic Royal Pavilion, built between 1815 and 1822. Other major Brighton landmarks are its two piers. The West Pier (below) was built in 1866. It has been closed since 1975. The town's other pier is the Palace – built in 1891 it attracts over two million visitors every year.

West Wittering *left*

This small town has survived much of the rapid development that blights many coastal towns. This is thanks to local campaigners who worked hard in the 1950s and 60s to preserve the natural beauty of the area. The beach and its surrounding marshland is still managed by a private local conservation charity in combination with English Nature. At low tide over half a mile of sand is exposed, making this one of the least commercialised sandy beaches within easy reach of London.

Hayling Island *below*

The shingle beach at Hayling Island, just off the coast of Hampshire, is relatively new: it was previously a long sandy beach which has now been filled with stones to prevent erosion. The island is ten miles square and is shaped like an inverted capital "T"; it is connected to the mainland by a road bridge. Hayling is a popular holiday destination and famous among watersports enthusiasts as being the place where windsurfing was invented. Its waters are clean and the foreshore at West Beachlands has European Blue Flag accreditation. In 1996 the historic oysterbeds on the north-west coast of Hayling Island were restored by the local council, creating a wildlife haven. "Hayling" is a Saxon word meaning "Hegel's People"; before they settled the Romans left their mark, building at least one structure on the northern part of the island. Sailing is very popular on Hayling and many Olympic competitors train here.

Selsey *left*

First opened in 1860, the lifeboat station at Selsey is a striking structure along this part of the West Sussex coastline. Selsey's name derives from "seal island" – a reminder that it lies on the narrow Manhood Peninsula, a small island almost cut off from the mainland by the sea. The museum, adjacent to the lifeboat station, charts the history of Selsey and its lifeboats. Erosion and periodic flooding are a continual problem for this area which was once reliant on its fishing industries. Today the town's fortunes are tied up with tourism; the road into the town is particularly busy during the summer season.

Alum Bay *left*

Adjacent to the Needles, Alum Bay is another part of this coast affected by severe erosion. Climbing the attractive sandstone cliffs was once a popular pastime but the crumbling state of the rocks today makes this hazardous. The Bay's famous coloured sand is collected when there are cliff falls and sold in glass containers. Alum Bay once had a pier on the beach but it was damaged in 1927 and not repaired. During the summer season a popular chairlift takes tourists down to the beach below – the energetic can walk down a flight of 188 steps!

The Needles *below*

The row of stacks known as the Needles are one of the best-known and most spectacular sights along the south coast. They take their name from a sharp stone called Lot's Wife that used to stand there until it fell down in a storm in 1764. There has long been a military presence on the cliffs near the Needles with batteries of cannon placed there to protect the western approach to the Solent – the stretch of water between the Isle of Wight and the mainland coast. The Needles Lighthouse was constructed in 1855 at sea-level, replacing the 1786 cliff-top lighthouse.

Portsmouth *above*

Portsmouth is a busy city on the Hampshire coast, with a population of about 190,000. Its history and fortunes are intertwined with that of the Royal Navy; it is home to a major dockyard and its economy is reliant on commercial maritime operations. The town's growth began in the 12th century following the building of an Augustinian Priory at Southwick. It became an established port during the reign of King John (1199-1216) and it was frequently the launchpad for attacks on France. The first fortifications in Portsmouth were built by Henry V. The Round Tower is a later addition to the town's defences – built in stone by order of Henry VIII. One of the town's most famous attractions dates from his reign – the flagship *The Mary Rose* which sank in the harbour in 1545 and was salvaged in 1984. Many historic ships including *HMS Warrior* (above), the world's first iron-hulled battleship, built in 1860, are on display.

South-West England

The towns and villages of south-west England may seem benign today but most have darker histories, featuring the worst of human activities – war, smuggling and wrecking. Grim times surrendered eventually to respectability thanks in large part to the railways that opened up the coast to Victorian holidaymakers, making tourist spots and artists' colonies of places previously known only for their poverty, isolation and toughness of life. Today the tremendous legacy of this coast is there for everyone to experience, coupled with scenery which ranges from the grandeur of Dorset's Jurassic coast to the beautiful bays of Cornwall.

Chesil Beach *right*
Chesil Beach, or Chesil Bank, is one of the greatest examples of the geological formation known as a "tombolo" in the world. This is a spit of land formed by longshore drift that has over time completely sealed in a section of coast, creating a number of lagoons. It is 17 miles long and has been built up by the steady deposition of flint and chert pebbles – the bulkiest towards Portland and the smaller ones at the Abbotsbury end of the bar.

Old Harry *above*
Old Harry is a chalk stack that marks the point were the Purbeck Hills fall into the sea on the Dorset coast below Ballard Down. Old Harry is about 200 years old. "He" used to be permanently accompanied by a smaller stump called Old Harry's Wife, but "she" collapsed in the 1950s and only reappears during the low spring tides. The name "Old Harry" refers to the devil who is said to have rested on the rock.

Durdle Door *right*
Lulworth Cove is a horseshoe-shaped natural harbour on the Dorset coast, which attracts thousands of visitors each year. The cove is famous for its geology with the "folded strata" that forms it clearly visible. The local environment supports a wide variety of natural species including one unique species of butterfly – the Lulworth Skipper, discovered near the natural arch Durdle Door in 1832.

Golden Cap *above*

If ever there was a spot to sit and stare then it is on the Golden Cap – the stretch of coast between the towns of Bridport and Lyme Regis. Here the cliffs reach their highest point along the entire south coast of England climbing to 650ft (192m). The beaches below the Golden Cap are famous for their fossils but can be hazardous and are subject to rock falls. They are also swamped at high tide and unwary fossil-hunters should always guard against the risk of being caught and stranded.

Lyme Regis *left*

Lyme Regis is one of the best known coastal towns in Dorset and is famous for the Cobb, a pier which projects out into Lyme Bay and forms a harbour. Lyme Regis has strong literary associations, featuring in Jane Austen's *Northanger Abbey* and *Persuasion*, and John Fowles' *The French Lieutenant's Woman*.

Torquay *right*

Torquay is the best-known of Torbay's "English Riviera" towns. Its history may stretch back over 1,000 years but its current fortunes owe the most to its popularity as a resort in the late 18th and early 19th centuries. It first came to prominence when naval officers stationed here during the Napoleonic Wars spread the word of its pleasant climate and aspect. Torquay is closely associated with crime-writer Agatha Christie, who was born here in 1890. Today there is a specially devised walk that allows visitors to combine sightseeing with a little amateur sleuthing.

Dartmouth *right*

Famous for its naval training college, which all officers of the Royal Navy attend, Dartmouth is situated on the banks of the river Dart. Its deep waters have allowed a strategic harbour to be developed. It was from here that Richard the Lionheart's armies set off for the Crusades in the 12th century, and it has also been subject to attack – twice during the 100 Years War against France in the 14th century after which a huge chain was placed across the Dart to prevent such raids. One of the town's most famous sites is the old wharf of Bayard's Cove. Its 18th-century buildings have featured in a number of TV series including the long-running *Onedin Line*.

Start Point *left*

This isolated peninsula projects nearly a mile out into the sea and marks the southern end of Start Bay which runs from here to Dartmouth. This can be a bleak spot and has been the site of many shipwrecks; a lighthouse was built here in 1836.

Plymouth *below*

With its spectacular natural harbour, Plymouth lies at the mouths of two rivers – the Plym and the Tamar. It has been home to two Royal Naval bases and is associated with many of the most famous figures in England's maritime history. In the 16th century the merchant Sir William Hawkins and his son Sir John Hawkins established the grim triangle trade from Plymouth, exchanging manufactured goods for West African slaves and transporting them to the Spanish colonies in Central and South America. Plymouth has seen some famous arrivals and departures. The American Indian princess Pocahontas landed in Plymouth in 1616 and it was from here that *The Mayflower* departed to set up the Plymouth Colony in America in 1620. The city's military importance resulted in heavy bombing during the war – in all 1,172 people were killed in air raids. Plymouth is currently undergoing a process of urban redevelopment.

Falmouth *left*

One of Cornwall's gems, Falmouth is a picturesque town, with many seafaring connections. It was from here that a number of successful round-the-world yachting attempts have begun or ended including those of Sir Francis Chichester and Dame Ellen MacArthur. The town is protected by Pendennis Castle, completed in 1540. The castle was one of the last fortified places in England to fall to parliamentary forces during the Civil War. News of victory at the Battle of Trafalgar and Nelson's death came ashore here from the schooner *Pickle*. Falmouth has featured in a number of films including the 1950 version of *Treasure Island*.

St Michael's Mount *below*

Linked to the mainland by its regularly submerged causeway, St Michael's Mount deserves to rank among the most spectacular and romantic spots anywhere along the British coast. It has been a priory, fortress, a place of pilgrimage and, since 1659, a private home belonging to the St Aubyn family. It is now one of the National Trust's most visited sites.

Land's End *left*

This is the most westerly point on mainland Britain. The Longships lighthouse lies within sight of the shore, located on an island of the same name. In Arthurian legend, the halfway point between Land's End and the Isles of Scilly is where the mythical land of Lyonesse was located before the ocean swallowed it up. Land's End is the meeting place of the north and south sections of the Cornish coastal footpath.

Newlyn *below*

Life in Newlyn has traditionally centred on its harbour and fishing fleet. The town was home to William Lovett, one of the leaders of the Chartist Movement which was dedicated to bringing about electoral reform in Britain. It is also known for the Newlyn riots in 1896 caused by the local fishermen – strong sabbatarians all – taking exception to crews from the north of England landing fish on Sunday. In the 1890s the town was adopted by a group of artists, later to be known as the Newlyn School.

St Ives *above and left*

St Ives derives its name from Saint Ia who is said to have arrived here in the fifth century from Ireland. It is an exquisite seaside town bounded by two sandy beaches and provides visitors with experiences far beyond those of the usual seaside resorts thanks to the town's rich artistic heritage. St Ives' fortunes once rested upon its fishing industry. Now it relies on tourism boosted by the presence of no less than two significant art museums including a branch of the Tate (left). The town is associated with Ben Nicholson, Barbara Hepworth and Naum Gabo who all settled here, forming one of the 20th century's most significant artists' colonies anywhere in Britain. It was also the home of Bernard Leach – a key figure in modern art pottery.

Bedruthan Steps *below*

In spring, pink fields of thrift soften the tops of the cliffs overlooking Bedruthan Steps – a set of granite stacks that emerge some 200ft (61m) from the sea. Bedruthan was a legendary giant fabled for using the steps as a causeway.

Uphill near Weston-super-Mare *above*

The small village of Uphill is situated just outside the busy seaside resort of Weston-super-Mare. It was settled long before the Roman invasion and it thrived under the Romans too, probably as a fort. Its most venerable building is the Old Church of St Nicholas which was built around 1066, probably on the site of an earlier Saxon church. For centuries it has been a landmark for sailors navigating the dangerous currents of the bay.

Porlock *above*

A spectacular view from Exmoor across Porlock to the coast and the Bristol Channel. The little village of Porlock nestles in a hollow below Exmoor; access to the village is via Porlock Hill, a road with a series of hairpin bends and a 1-in-4 gradient. Near the sea is Porlock Ridge and Saltmarsh nature reserve, a Site of Special Scientific Interest created when the lowland behind a high shingle embankment was breached by the sea in the 1990s. Two miles west of the village within beautiful woodland is the church of St Culborne – just 35ft long, it is the smallest church in England. Porlock has strong associations with the Romantic poets – William Wordsworth and Samuel Taylor Coleridge roamed the North Somerset countryside, and after one of his epic walks Coleridge had a vision in which a "person from Porlock" appeared before him; when transcribed, it became 54 lines of *Kubla Khan*, one of his most famous poems.

Lundy *left*

Located off the north Devon coast Lundy is the site of England's only marine nature reserve. For many centuries it was a lawless place – a refuge for pirates who preyed on traffic in the Bristol Channel. Lundy only gained respectability when it was bought by the Heaven family in the 1830s. In 1969 Lundy became the responsibility of the Landmark Trust. The island is rich in wildlife – particularly seabirds and mammals including the pygmy shrew. Its name derives from the Norse for a puffin.

East Anglia and Lincolnshire

Wide open skies, reed-fringed marshes and magnificent beaches characterise the coastline of East Anglia and Lincolnshire, from Essex to the Humber. The Essex coastline is dotted with creeks and river valleys graced with beautiful towns and villages such as Maldon and Tollesbury. The Suffolk coast has some of the best seaside resorts in Britain – with Aldeburgh, Southwold and Walberswick among them. The vast network of overlapping waterways and lakes of the Broads provide Norfolk with a unique landscape while to the north, the "quiet beauty" of the Lincolnshire coast has provided inspiration for artists and writers, including the poet John Betjeman.

Brightlingsea *top*

The ancient port of Brightlingsea lies at the mouth of the river Colne. One of its earliest roles was the defence of Colchester, further up the river, and it is the only Cinque Port north of the Thames. Today it is a typical south-east seaside resort with colourful beach huts, a children's paddling pool and a sandy beach. Its main industry was fishing and the town's local oysters were sought after. It is very popular with recreational sailors and the Brightlingsea Sailing Club has an active membership.

Tollesbury *below*

A row of weatherboarded sail lofts at Tollesbury, situated on the mouth of the Blackwater estuary, east of Maldon. The village signpost shows a plough and a sail; the sail lofts are a potent reminder that the village has derived as much benefit from the sea as agriculture over the centuries. The village featured in the 2006 BBC series *Restoration Village* for its efforts to restore the listed Woodrolfe Granary, a weatherboarded building overlooking the estuary and saltmarshes.

Shingle Street *right*

South of Aldeburgh, on the Suffolk Heritage Coast, the tiny hamlet of Shingle Street is a bleak spot with a mysterious history. Nearby Orford Ness was used for all sorts of clandestine military activities from the 1930s up until the 1960s. During the Second World War Shingle Street was evacuated and the area heavily mined. It was at Orford Ness that radar was first tested.

Maldon *below*

Located east of Colchester on the Blackwater estuary, the historic town of Maldon was, for centuries, one of just two towns in the county of Essex. King Edward the Elder lived here in the eighth century while Danish settlers were intent on over-running the whole of East Anglia; the Old English epic poem *The Battle of Maldon* chronicles the Anglo-Saxon defeat in AD991 by a force of invading Vikings. The battle is commemorated by a bronze statue, erected in 2006, of Byrhtnoth, the Saxon warrior who perished in the battle. Maldon is the home of the famous brown-sailed Thames sailing barges.

Snape Maltings *left*

The Maltings at Snape consist of a magnificent collection of 19th-century granaries and malthouses on the banks of the river Alde. Originally used for the brewing of beer, the maltings closed in 1960. They have since been converted into a world-class concert hall in which the main events of the annual Aldeburgh Festival are staged. Nearby is the Holst Library named after Imogen, the daughter of composer Gustav Holst. She was a friend of Benjamin Britten, the founder with Peter Pears of the Aldeburgh Festival and its artistic director from 1956 to 1977.

Sizewell *inset*

This small fishing village near Thorpeness is the location of two nuclear power stations – Sizewell A and Sizewell B. Sizewell A started to generate power in 1966 and houses two 1000 megawatt Magnox reactors. It is reaching the end of its life and is due to be decommissioned at a cost of over £1bn. Sizewell B is the UK's only large pressurised water reactor and was built between 1988 and 1995. The dome of Sizewell B still packs a dramatic punch when observed from a distance down the coast.

Cromer *right*

Well into the 19th century Cromer, on the north coast of Norfolk, was little more than a fishing village; it became fashionable in the early 19th century when a clutch of rich Norwich banking families made it their summer home. The development of the railway hastened Cromer's expansion, bringing visitors keen to enjoy its beautiful beaches. Today Cromer is famous for its pier and its seafood – the Cromer crab is a famous local delicacy. The parish church of St Peter and St Paul dominates the skyline – it has a magnificent Burne-Jones stained-glass window, plus modern stained-glass commemorating the town's seafarers; its 160ft (49m) tower is the highest in the county. Cromer is renowned for its two lifeboats which, over the years, have carried out a number of significant rescues.

Hunstanton *left*

"Sunny Hunny" as it is known locally is a popular seaside town in Norfolk on the easternmost lip of the Wash. Because it faces west it is the only English east coast resort to enjoy sunsets over the sea. Hunstanton is famous for its colourful striped cliffs, a combination of reddish sandstone topped by chalk. This unique cliff formation is popular with fossil-hunters.

Mundesley *below left*

A wooden groyne projects across the beach and into the sea near Mundesley – a small village on Norfolk's north-east coast. It was once an important port and a popular Victorian resort but coastal erosion has destroyed the railway connection and the beach is littered with sections of fallen track. Mundesley's war memorial celebrates the sailors and volunteers who cleared the North Sea of mines during and after the Second World War.

Morston Marshes *below*

This atmospheric part of the north Norfolk coast is protected by the National Trust; it consists of a maze of creeks and mudflats supporting maritime plants such as sea lavender and attracts many birds. Spring migrants include chiffchaffs, wheatears and sandwich terns. By the end of April the reedbed is full of reed and sedge warblers while the extended autumn migration sees the pools occupied by green and wood sandpiper, greenshank, whimbrel and little ringed plover.

Terrington Marsh *above*

Terrington Marsh is a tranquil spot to the south of the Wash. Its main local settlement is Terrington St Clement – extending over 13 square miles, it is said to be the largest village in Norfolk. In the Second World War an entirely bogus airfield was created on Terrington Marsh using an elaborate array of lights as a decoy target for German bombers seeking the nearby real airfield at Sutton Bridge. It was a highly successful ploy and Terrington Marsh was bombed heavily on a number of occasions, with no cost to military infrastructure – the only damage being to local potato fields.

Skegness *right*

Low winter sun casts a warm light over the beach at Skegness in winter. To the south is the nature reserve at Gibraltar Point, an area of unspoilt coastline with important plant and animal communities. The coastline here is of great scientific interest and is made up of sandy and muddy seashore, sand dune, saltmarsh and freshwater habitats. The reserve extends for a distance of about three miles along the coast from the southern end of Skegness to the entrance to the Wash.

Yorkshire

The Yorkshire coast's remarkable "craggy grandeur" makes it both inspiring and dangerous. Historically its villages and towns thrived on the sea industries of fishing, whaling and smuggling. With the arrival of the railways in Victorian times seaside visitors flocked to the coast, followed by artists and writers. Today, the coastline that forms the eastern edge of the North York Moors national park has been re-branded as the North Yorkshire Heritage Coast. The Cleveland Way long-distance footpath hugs the clifftops from Saltburn in the north to Filey in the south.

Flamborough Head *left*
Thornwick Nab *above*

Jutting out into the North Sea and home to large populations of seabirds, the seven-mile long headland at Flamborough Head between Filey and Bridlington is one of the North Yorkshire coastline's best-known natural wonders. A benign spot on a warm summer day, this can be a ferocious part of the coast and has been the site of numerous shipwrecks. In 1674 the decision was taken to build a lighthouse, which is Britain's oldest. It is the only known example of a beacon lighthouse in England, where a huge brazier on top would be used as a light. There is no evidence it was ever used, and a new lighthouse was built on the cliffs in 1806. It was just off the coast in 1779 that the US sea commander John Paul Jones made his name in an engagement with British ships during the American War of Independence, managing to capture the Royal Naval vessel *The Countess of Scarborough*. At low tide beneath the cliffs at nearby Nab Close (above) a spectacular wave-cut platform is exposed.

Scarborough *above*

Its stunning location and sandy beaches meant that Scarborough was well-placed to become Britain's first seaside resort. The Grand Hotel was completed in 1867 and was, at the time, one of the largest hotels in the world. Its four towers represented the seasons and its 12 floors the months of the year. The town dates back to the mid-

10th century. It suffered from Viking raids and was burnt down prior to the Norman invasion, only recovering in the reign of Edward II. In the middle ages the famous Scarborough Fair lasted for six weeks and people flocked to it from all over Europe. The headland with the ruined Norman castle separates North Bay from the South.

Whitby *left*

Named as Best Seaside Resort 2006 by *Holiday Which* magazine, Whitby has a long history. The town's first major structure was religious – an abbey was built and Whitby later became a centre of learning thanks to its first abbess Hilda. By early modern times the town's fortunes were more commercial – the export of coal and alum. It was also a shipbuilding centre and, by the late 18th century, a thriving whaling port. It was in Whitby that Captain James Cook, the naval explorer, learned the maritime trade and there is a museum dedicated to him in the town. The view (left) is across the harbour to St Mary's church and the ruins of the abbey.

Staithes *above*

Known locally as "Steers", Staithes is a seaside village at the most northerly point of the North Yorkshire coast. Once a thriving fishing port, Staithes now relies mainly on tourism. The village has a reputation as an artists' colony and was even home to its own "group", known as the Northern Impressionists, which included Dame Laura Knight. Staithes' most famous son was Captain Cook who worked here as a grocer's apprentice between 1745-1746.

Boggle Hole *left*

Half a mile south of the picturesque fishing village of Robin Hood's Bay lies Boggle Hole, a wonderful place to search for fossils and explore rock pools.

North-East England

The coastline of north-east England stretches from the Scottish border to the banks of the river Tees. In between it encompasses the estuaries of the rivers Tees, Wear and Tyne including the industrial heartlands of Middlesbrough, Sunderland and Newcastle. To the north lies the beautiful unspoilt countryside of Northumberland, which includes the stunning castles of Dunstanburgh and Bamburgh, and the exquisite Lindisfarne, with its castle and ruined priory.

Saltburn-by-the-Sea *above*
One of Saltburn's greatest attractions is its beautifully renovated pier. This pretty town was laid out by Henry Pease who, in 1859, had a vision of a planned seaside resort when walking along the cliffs at Saltburn. Over the next few years Pease rebuilt the town giving the streets names such as Ruby, Emerald and Pearl.

Roker Pier *left*
The view south-east from Sunderland shows the red and white Roker lighthouse and pier almost entirely obscured during a violent storm. The lighthouse was built in 1903 at the instructions of the Earl of Durham.

Whitburn Coastal Park *below*
The wind and sea-etched cliffs along the South Tyneside coast (now the Whitburn Coastal Park) are testament to serious coastal erosion. Once the village of Marsden stood here but when Whitburn Colliery closed in 1968 the decision was taken to demolish the village as it lay in the path of the retreating cliffs.

Dunstanburgh *above*

There can be few more spectacular sights on the English coastline than the ruins of 14th-century Dunstanburgh Castle. It was once one of the most formidable strongholds in the north and its grandeur is still apparent despite its ruinous state. One of the best ways to reach the castle today is across the rocky beach; on rougher days the wind and sea provide a suitable accompaniment to this magnificent scene.

Bamburgh Castle *left*

The impregnable stronghold of Bamburgh Castle is perched on a huge rock, visible for miles around on the Northumbrian coast. It dominates the pretty village, which clusters around the castle. The local churchyard has a monument to Grace Darling, together with the graves of victims of shipwrecks on the nearby Farne Islands. Bamburgh was the tribal stronghold of an ancient British tribe called the *Votadini* who stood out against the Vikings. The name originates from the time of Aethelfrith, the first King of Northumbria, who named the fortress or "burgh" after his wife, Bebba. Bamburgh Castle was heavily restored during Victoria's reign by the Newcastle-born industrialist William, Lord Armstrong. In 1971 Bamburgh was chosen as Macbeth's stronghold in the film version of the play directed by Roman Polanski.

Lindisfarne *inset*

To the north of Bamburgh lies Holy Island or Lindisfarne (to use its more ancient name) seen here with its dramatic castle. Lindisfarne is separated from the mainland at high tides and can only be reached by its causeway. The Norman priory stands on the site of an Anglo-Saxon monastery founded by St Aidan in 635. Aidan is believed to have chosen the island because of its isolation and proximity to the Northumbrian capital at Bamburgh; it proved a strategic spot from which he could launch his campaign to convert Northumberland to Christianity. In the mid 7th century Cuthbert became the fifth bishop of Lindisfarne and further built the island's reputation thanks to his ability to heal the sick and work miracles. The castle was converted into a private residence by Sir Edwin Lutyens in 1903. It has been a National Trust property since 1944.

Wales

Few regions of Britain can boast such a beautiful and varied coastline within a relatively compact area. In the north, the popular seaside resorts of Llandudno, Prestatyn and Colwyn Bay rub shoulders with fortified towns such as Caernarfon and Conwy. In the west there are remote beaches with historic centres such as Harlech and St David's. In the south, the Gower peninsula between Llanelli and Swansea was the first place in Britain to be designated as an Area of Outstanding Natural Beauty. And the great cities of Cardiff and Swansea, once marked by their industrial heritage, now boast highly acclaimed quayside developments with new landmark buildings and restored gems from the country's industrial past.

Swansea Bay *above*

The wide and expansive Swansea Bay (seen from a vantage point on Kilvey Hill) is an inlet of the Bristol Channel, stretching from Mumbles Head in the west to Port Talbot in the east. It was once an important area for fishing and its oysters were legendary, but in the early 20th century pollution and over-fishing destroyed the beds. The height of Swansea's fame came during the Industrial Revolution; in the 19th century it was the biggest exporter of coal in the world. But the city suffered in the Second World War and lost much of its historic centre. Today it is a vibrant and exciting city, proud of its cultural heritage – the new maritime quarter houses the National Waterfront Museum celebrating Wales' history of industry and innovation; every autumn the city hosts a festival in honour of Dylan Thomas, Swansea's most famous son.

Three Cliffs Bay *above left*

This beautiful bay on the Gower Peninsula is widely regarded as one of Britain's best. Located just to the west of Swansea, it takes its name from the three attractive limestone cliffs that jut out into the sea. The three stunning tracts of golden sand are all connected, but visitors can only walk from one to the other at low tide. The wind-battered ruins of Pennard Castle stand guard over the area on a nearby hill.

Tenby *left*

This pretty seaside town grew up around the now ruined remains of the castle which stands on a high rocky headland overlooking the resort's two beaches. Tenby has many interesting sights including its 13th-century town walls and a Tudor merchant's house. The fort on St Catherine's Island was built in the 1860s to guard against French invasion. Just off the coast lies Caldey Island, a reformed Cistercian monastery.

Worms Head, Rhossili *above*

With its three-mile long sandy beach, views out over Worms Head and frequent spectacular sunsets over the Atlantic, Rhossili Bay is one of the most dramatic stretches of Britain's coastline. The cliffs and beach are managed by the National Trust and so development here is restricted – the village consists of a church, a pub, and some tea rooms. The beach is reached by a stepped path behind the pub, while the best way to appreciate the whole sweep of the bay is to walk west over the soft, grazed grass to the tip of the headland. Worms Head is connected to the mainland by a causeway which is passable for two hours either side of low tide.

Fishguard *left*

The harbour at Fishguard is dotted with pleasure craft in this view from the south-east, taken from the heights above Goodwick Quay. The mouth of the river Gwaun around which the town has grown up can just be seen to the right of the photograph. The town, as its name implies, was once an important fishing centre and had a very active herring fleet. Its harbour is now the place to catch ferries to Rosslare in Ireland. In 1797 an ill-conceived and poorly-executed French invasion of Britain finally petered out in Fishguard with the surrender being signed by the French commander, an American called Colonel William Tate, in the Royal Oak pub.

St Justinian's *right*

Legend has it that the body of St Justinian – the Byzantine emperor and saint – was brought to Wales and landed here on the Pembrokshire coast. There is a nearby chapel dedicated to him although there is no public access. Today, as well as being a spot for walkers and climbers, St Justinian's is important as the point of departure for summer ferries to the bird and grey seal colonies at Ramsay Island. St Justinian's is also home to the local lifeboat station – the red building in the photograph.

Portmeirion *right*

The Italianate village of Portmeirion owes its existence to the architect Sir Clough Williams-Ellis (1883-1978) who built the village on his own private peninsula on the coast of Snowdonia. Construction took 50 years, and many of the buildings incorporate important architectural features which Williams-Ellis rescued from buildings that were being demolished elsewhere. The grounds are criss-crossed with beautiful woodland walks. The main white building in the photograph is the hotel, which dates from 1850; in the distance is the Observatory Tower, designed in 1935. The 1960s television series *The Prisoner* was shot on location at Portmeirion.

Harlech *below*

The high ground to the east of Harlech provides tremendous views due west over the castle and out across Tremadog Bay. The construction of Harlech Castle began in 1283 during the reign of Edward I. It was one of the "iron ring" fortresses built around the Snowdonia coast to intimidate the Welsh into accepting English rule. Originally, the castle was immediately above the sea, but due to coastal retreat, the stairway called the "way from the sea" no longer descends to a beach. It was an important Lancastrian stronghold during the Wars of the Roses and the song *Men of Harlech* commemorates the seven-year seige of the castle between 1461-1468.

South Stack Lighthouse *right*

The South Stack lighthouse is situated on Holy Island on the north-west coast of Anglesey. It is considered to be one of the most magnificent lighthouses in Wales. Built in 1809, it has over 400 stone steps which lead down to the island where there is a superb view of the cliff face and the 4,000 pairs of seabirds nesting there during the summer. The Stack is reached via an aluminium bridge – far safer than the original basket and pulley system that transported lighthousemen in earlier years. Designed by Daniel Alexander, the beam of the lighthouse can be seen by ships 28 miles out to sea.

Barmouth *below*

The view due west from the small village of Penmaenpool takes in the broad sweep of the estuary of the river Mawddach. Penmaenpool has grown up at a bridging point over the river. Downstream, the Mawddach enters Cardigan Bay close to the exquisite seaside resort of Barmouth. In his account of walking trips in Wales, the poet William Wordsworth summed up Barmouth's attractions: "With a fine sea view in front, the mountains behind, the glorious estuary running eight miles inland, and Cadair Idris within compass of a day's walk, Barmouth can always hold its own against any rival". Notable buildings in the town include Ty Gwyn – a medieval tower house and the 18th-century Ty Crwn prison. There is also a new Lifeboat Visitor Centre.

Porth Cwyfan *right*

The 13th-century chapel of St Cwyfan perches on the island of Cribina, on the south-west coast of Anglesey. Known as the Church in the Sea, or by its Welsh name of Cwyfan, the chapel has been awarded a grant by Welsh Heritage to repair the roof, walls and windows and to limewash the interior. Elements of the chapel's 12th-century structure still survive, but most of it dates from the 14th century. It is still used for services and is a popular site for weddings.

Caernarfon Castle *above*

It took more than 50 years to construct Caernarfon Castle. The main period of work began in 1283 and went on until 1323. This formidable building was part of the post-war settlement of north Wales following Edward I's successful campaign against the forces of Llywelyn ap Gruffydd in 1277. Its construction cost £22,000 – an enormous sum at the time, equivalent to more than a year's income for the royal treasury. The castle, designed by James St George, was said to have been inspired by the walls of Constantinople – something that prominent crusader Edward I would have appreciated. The tradition of naming the heir to the English throne the Prince of Wales originated here when Edward I offered the Welsh a successor who did not speak a word of English, only to reveal he meant his baby son Edward to inherit his powers in Wales.

Conwy *above*

Conwy is one of Europe's finest examples of a medieval walled town. Conwy Castle was built by Edward I between 1283 to 1289 and, together with the castles and walls of Harlech, Caernarfon and Beaumaris, is a World Heritage Site. An estimated £15,000 was spent building the castle and the town's defences. Another of Conwy's tourist attractions is the 1826 Conwy Suspension Bridge built by Thomas Telford over the river Conwy next to the castle. It is claimed that the marshy ground at Conwy Morfa nearby is the place that golf was first played in Wales. It was also where Hugh Iorys Hughes developed and later built the famous floating Mulberry Harbour, used in the invasion of Europe in the Second World War.

North-West England

The north-west coast of England takes in the bright lights of Blackpool, the beautifully restored Merseyside docks, the open sands of Cumbria and the rocky coastline of the Isle of Man with its lighthouses and haunted castles. On this coast the Romans posted garrisons, smugglers and wreckers carried out their dubious trades and racehorses have thundered up and down the sands at Southport in training for the Grand National.

Caldy Beach *right*

This view looks north-east across the sands of New Brighton – with the breakwater and Perch Rock lighthouse in view. The line of docks at Bootle can just be seen in the far distance. The 19th century saw New Brighton's transition from a place with a reputation for smuggling and wrecking to one that promised fun and relaxation for holidaymakers. At Caldy Island on the Wirral coast, the groynes loom like strange sentinels. Beyond them, to the west, is a view of the mountains of north Wales across the river Dee.

The Mersey from New Brighton *left*

There is no better way to experience Liverpool and Merseyside than from the deck of the famous Mersey ferry. In the 19th century Liverpool became known as the "second port of the Empire" after London, but it suffered badly from the post-war economic decline. Its fortunes have improved in recent years and since 1995 Liverpool has experienced quite startling growth, including the complete overhaul of its waterfront which was declared a World Heritage Site in 2004. Here the view east shows the bronze domes of the Royal Liver Building which, together with the Cunard and Port of Liverpool buildings, form the "Three Graces" of the city's skyline.

Blackpool *right*

The UK's premier seaside resort, Blackpool's name is probably derived from the black peaty water which flowed into the Irish Sea across an area of marsh at this point on the coast. The town's fortunes are inextricably linked to tourism and most of its sites are associated with it, including the famous Blackpool Tower built in 1894. If it seems familiar then it should – this striking landmark is a scaled-down replica of the Eiffel Tower. Another much photographed attraction is the double-decker "balloon buses" that ply the promenade. Blackpool has traditionally been the resort of choice for Lancashire city-dwellers and Glaswegians.

Ravenglass *left*

The view south-east from Saltcoats on the Cumbrian coast shows Ravenglass spread out along the estuary created by the confluence of three local rivers – the Esk, Mite and Irt. Known as Glannaventa to the Romans, this was an important garrison site for over 300 years.

Peel, Isle of Man
below

Linked by a causeway to Peel, Peel Castle stands on tiny St Patrick's Island. It was built in the 11th century by the Vikings, in the reign of King Magnus Barelegs. Like many other buildings in the town it is built of red standstone, giving rise to Peel being called "the rose city" because of the gorgeous hues that play on the stone in sunlight. Peel is also the location for the island's only cathedral – St German's. Completed in 1884, its diocese not only includes the islands of Sodor and Man, but also the Hebridean islands off the west coast of Scotland.

Scotland

From the border north of Berwick in the east, to the beautiful island of Arran in the west, the Scottish coast is stunning in the variety of its landscape. Rocky outcrops are dotted with magnificent castles, while the rugged coastline provided natural harbours where fishing villages could develop. The Orkneys, Shetlands and the Western Isles are full of varied coastal scenery – stacks, arches, towering sea cliffs, sandy beaches and dunes all providing a wonderful natural habitat for birds and plants. But Scotland's coast is also the site of many beautiful towns – from the home of golf at St Andrews to splendid west coast islands such as Skye and Harris, this is a coastline rich in history and full of interest for the visitor.

Tantallon Castle *above*

This stronghold was once the first major obstacle any army venturing across Scotland's easternmost border would have encountered. Tantallon Castle is just three miles from North Berwick and its vantage on top of a high cliff gives it an unimpeded view of the Bass Rock in the Firth of Forth. Built in 1358, Tantallon's fortunes finally declined in 1651 when Cromwell destroyed it while rooting out bandits who had been using it as a base.

Forth Bridges *top*

In the foreground is the mammoth structure of the Forth Rail Bridge, built between 1883-1890 to connect Edinburgh and Fife. Regarded as an engineering marvel, it was constructed at some cost to human life. Of the 4,600 people employed to build it, 63 people are thought to have died and hundreds of others were injured. In the distance are the sleek lines of the Forth Road Bridge, built in 1964. When opened, it was the largest suspension bridge in the world and together with the approach viaducts it is over one and a half miles long. The main towers extend 512ft (156m) above the river and the sag of the cables between the towers is approximately 300ft (91m).

St Andrews *left*

Despite being named after the apostle Saint Andrew, the first holy figure associated with this site is Kenneth, who established a monastery here in the 6th century. Today, St Andrews is host to Scotland's oldest university and also enjoys an international reputation as the "home of golf". It is here that The Royal and Ancient Golf Club has its headquarters – one of the oldest and most beautiful courses in the world and the frequent location of the Open Championship, the oldest of the four big golf competitions held annually. The view is of the ruins of the Cathedral of St Andrew, once one of Scotland's largest buildings.

Duncansby Head *right*

Near the inland village of John O'Groats, Duncansby Head, with its remarkable stacks, is the most northerly spot on the north-east coast of Scotland. The Stacks of Duncansby and Thirle Door Arch are truly dramatic – especially with the air around them filled with the movement and sound of the large colonies of seabirds here. Duncansby Head is also the site of a lighthouse built in 1924. This beautiful stretch of coastline is reached via a single-track road from John O'Groats; on arrival, visitors are rewarded with views north over Orkney and west to Dunnet Head, the most northerly point on mainland Britain. A short walk behind the lighthouse and the view opens up to the south, over the Stacks and the Arch.

Old Man of Hoy, Orkney *above*

Situated approximately 10 miles north of the Caithness coast, the Orkneys are a group of around 70 islands containing some of the most dramatic cliffs and rock formations in Britain. Mainland is the largest of the group, followed by Hoy. The Old Man of Hoy is a sandstone rock stack rising from the sea to a height of 450ft (137m) off the west coast of Hoy and is considered a classic challenge by rock climbers. The first successful ascent was televised in 1966. Modern techniques and equipment, however, have made it more accessible to slightly less experienced climbers and it has now been conquered many times. The Old Man of Hoy's days may be numbered as it takes a terrific beating from the sea and prevailing wind each winter. Eventually, like all such stacks it can be expected to crumble and fall into the surrounding sea due to coastal erosion.

Dunnottar Castle *left*

The ruins of the medieval fortress of Dunnottar Castle, near Stonehaven, stand guard over the sea. This was home to the Keith clan and was used as a secure place in times of strife for the Scottish crown jewels. The ruins are spread over a three acre area virtually surrounded by 160ft (50m) high sheer cliffs. In 1990 Dunnottar was used as the key location in the Mel Gibson and Glenn Close screen version of *Hamlet*.

Old Man Of Storr *left*

There are few more famous spots in western Scotland than the Storr – a rocky hill on the Trotternish peninsula overlooking the Sound of Raasay. The hill consists of a number of wonderfully shaped pinnacles or volcanic plugs.

Harris *right*

In Scottish Gaelic Harris – the southern part of the largest of the Outer Hebridean islands – is known as *Na Hearadh*. The northern part of the island is called Lewis. The photograph is taken on the west coast of South Harris, the side that faces the North Atlantic and which is blessed with some of the best beaches in Scotland. Among its main settlements is Rodel with the medieval kirk of St Clement's. One of the main tourist routes on Harris is the "Golden Road", which hugs the south-east coast from Tarbert to Rodel. It is so-named because of the high cost of its construction through difficult terrain.

Plockton *right*

Looking due north over the seaward end of Loch Carron on the north-west coast of Scotland to the pretty village of Plockton. This was a planned village established in the 18th century in an attempt to stem the flood of Scottish emigration. The village is a popular tourist resort, especially since it was chosen as the location of the television series *Hamish Macbeth*. Nearby is Duncraig Castle, a 19th-century stately home built by the Matheson family.

The Cuillins *below*

This photograph across Loch Scavaig shows the Cuillins in all their magnificence. They have been described as the most dramatic range in Britain and are much visited by walkers and climbers; for the less intrepid there are sightseeing boat trips from Elgol.

Isle of Arran *below*

This is the seventh largest Scottish island and it lies in the Firth of Clyde. The north of the island is a mountainous place with at least one peak, Goat Fell, reaching above 2,600ft (800m). It has been referred to as "Scotland in miniature" as it is divided into "Highland" and "Lowland" areas. There are many stone circles and standing stones dating from Neolithic times, including the standing stones on Machrie Moor and the Giant's Graves above Whiting Bay. The picturesque 16th-century Lochranza Castle is situated on the north coast of Arran. It was the hunting lodge of Scottish kings.

Isle of Jura *below*

The word *jura* is thought to derive from the Old Norse word for deer. This is appropriate, as Jura today supports a large population of red deer. The photograph shows the car ferry that operates across the Sound of Islay between Islay and Feolin Ferry on Jura. Jura is dominated by three steep-sided conical mountains on its western side – the Paps of Jura which rise to over 2,500ft (762m). Its west coast is home to a number of raised beaches – left high and dry by shifts in the sea level or even uplifted by earthquakes. It was on Jura that the novelist George Orwell completed his masterpiece *Nineteen Eighty-Four*.

Northern Ireland

The Antrim coast road of Northern Ireland is said to be one of the most scenic routes in the British Isles; inaccessible for years, when the coast road was built visitors flocked in droves, the highlight being the natural phenomenon of the Giant's Causeway. For much of its length the coast is flanked with towering cliffs, intersected with villages, waterfalls and the famous Glens of Antrim, beautiful wooded valleys which penetrate inland. From much of this coast the Mull of Kintyre and the islands of Scotland are visible – this is the narrowest strait in the British Isles and the geography bears testimony to the intertwined history of the two countries.

Carrick-a-Rede *above*

A woman pauses before taking the first step over the 80ft (24m) deep chasm between Carrick Island and the mainland of County Antrim. The rope bridge she must venture across was first placed here by fishermen to inspect their salmon nets. The bridge is now open to anyone walking the coastal path. Once they reach the predominantly limestone Carrick Island, visitors are rewarded with fine views of the Scottish islands and also the many seabirds that use the cliffs here for nesting and sanctuary.

Dunluce Castle *above*

On the Antrim coast between Portballintrae and Portrush, Dunluce is one of the most dramatic medieval ruined castles in Ireland. Dunluce transferred from English to Irish ownership in 1584 when it became the stronghold of the MacDonnell clan – the eventual Earls of Antrim. They improved the castle using the proceeds from the sale of goods seized from a Spanish ship (part of the Armada) wrecked nearby. After the Battle of the Boyne in 1690 the MacDonnells were unable to maintain the castle and it steadily became a ruin with much of its stone removed for nearby construction.

Giant's Causeway *right*

Located north of the town of Bushmills on the Antrim coast, the Giant's Causeway is an area of 40,000 interlocking basalt columns resulting from volcanic activity over 60 million years ago. The legend associated with this dramatic spot attributes the site to the giant Fionn mac Cumhail who built it to walk to Scotland in order to smite a Scottish giant called Benandonner. The same eruptions that created the Causeway are responsible for the geology of Fingal's Cave in Scotland. The Causeway is a World Heritage Site and was voted the fourth greatest natural wonder in the British Isles.

First published in 2009
by Myriad Books Limited,
35 Bishopsthorpe Road,
London SE26 4PA

Photographs copyright © Britain on View,
the image resource centre of Visit Britain

Text copyright © Jerome Monahan

Jerome Monahan has asserted his right under the Copyright, Designs and Patents Act 1998 to be identified as the author of this work.

ISBN 1 84746 252 9

EAN 978 1 84746 252 7

Designed by Jerry Goldie Graphic Design

Printed in China

www.myriadbooks.com